BUSINESS START-UP: FRANCHISING

[Franchising a Business Guide for Beginners]
(Business Start-up Ebook Series No. 6)

Dell Navarro

I'd like to dedicate this ebook to my mother, sisters, nephews, nieces and to all my friends. Thanks to Nicole, Samantha Mori and Hanna. Thank you for reading my ebooks. I hope you'll love my future published ebooks.

The Author

Dell Navarro

CONTENTS

Title Page	1
Dedication	3
Introduction	7
Chapter 1: Business Franchises	9
Chapter 2: Franchising Advantages	18
Chapter 3: Tips on Selecting the Best Franchises	27
Chapter 4: The Cost of Franchise and Personal Finance	37
Conclusion	45
About The Author	49
Books By This Author	51

INTRODUCTION

Welcome to this ebook titled
"BUSINESS START-UP: FRANCHISING"

[Franchising a Business Guide for Beginners]

(Business Start-up Ebook Series No. 6)

This is the 6th ebook in my Business Start-up Series. Other ebooks in this series are the following:

- Business Start-up: The Online Marketing

- Business Start-up: The Plan of Business

- Business Start-up: Branding

- Business Start-up: The Sales

- Business Start-up: Managing the Business

Everybody dreams to have a business that can easily be established and can return the capital investment in a short period of time. Franchising a brand is the best way of investing your capital fund. It is also the same with buying a business from an established and income generating company. A business company isn't usually for sale unless there's a difficulty in making sales and with negative net income. Buying a franchise will save you time in thinking a business that you like and what business is profitable. Save your years in building a brand name, a brand for franchise is already popular around the world. Start a company to operate your franchise or to hold more franchises. Like the franchisor, buying more franchises from numerous franchisors can give assurance that your investment fund is parked safely. Business success isn't only just a dream, it is realizable in franchising.

CHAPTER 1: BUSINESS FRANCHISES

A franchise is an authorization granted to a franchisee by a franchisor, the owner of a business being franchised with an agreement between the parties on payments of franchise fees. The franchisee establishes a business name to operate the franchise granted by owner franchisor. Franchise agreement allows the franchisee to use the brand name of the franchisor, the registered owner of the brand for franchise, sell products or services in the manners of the franchisor-owner. The franchisee should pay the total franchising fee for the purpose of establishing or construction of the business under franchise. Included also in the franchising fee, aside from the equipment, store or building, the initial merchandise for sale. The franchise agreement includes also the profit share in percentage from the total periodic sales or periodic net income of the franchisor. Other provision in the agreement may include training and support to franchisee to make the business operates in the manners of the franchisor.

Franchising is the fastest way of branching around a market territory without generating and investing a large capitalization. At the same time, the ownership of a franchise has the appearance of a branch store. The franchisees serve also as the ready sales customers of the franchisor. In a merchandising setup, the relationship between franchisor-franchisees is "wholesaler-retailers". Franchisor benefits on franchising agreement by transferring the management function to the franchisee. Each franchise is considered as an independent branch, operation and management costs are incurred and absorbed by each franchisee, franchisor is only to take its share from the profit or income of each franchise.

Franchising is favorable to franchisees as the latter take advantage of franchisor's marketable status, the franchisor's brand name is already established in the market. The franchisees can have the assurance of having a ready market, advertising is almost not important at the expense of the franchisees. In franchising, franchisor has the major responsibility in maintaining the brand's popularity and marketability. Franchising setup has the disadvantage of failure-chain-reaction, franchisees are dependent on the franchisor's marketability, if the needed promotion and advertising are not performed by franchisor, market patronage sways to other leading brands specially the other competing franchises. *Corona virus global pandemic is an example of a negative factor that has affected the fast food franchises, pandemic is a case that can't easily be solved by promotion and advertising.*

A franchisee business operator should view the franchise as an extension of franchisor's business, or its branch and should conform to its management style. Franchise should also be viewed as a profitable investment, there's an assurance of a return on investment.

On the other hand, buying a franchise can be frustrating if you don't like the nature of business and the franchisor's business doesn't have a large market niche. Like starting up a business, conduct a market research of a prospective franchise that you want to hold or specially if it's your first time to buy a franchise. Avoid holding franchises that will require you to manage more small units of store outlets (e.g. food carts), your reason of franchising should be to save time in starting up a business, of course investment depends on the size of your investment fund, food carts may require you to buy a food carts carrier, operating and management costs may go high and return may not be rewarding. Other importance of studying the market of any prospective franchise is to know the competitors of such franchise and its standing in the market. If it is the most popular franchise brand your chance to succeed is higher compared to other brands. If your investment fund isn't sufficient to cover the total franchise fees it is advisable to compare the other leading franchises. Avoid franchises with negative feedback from the market, with small number of stores and limited geographic presence.

Other Important Considerations on Franchising a Brand

1. Make sure that everybody knows the franchise that you want to buy. If the brand is popular, there's no problem with the market. There's an assurance of return on investment in few years time.

2. Know if other franchisees are not sell-

ing their existing franchises. Leaving the business is an indicator of loss from investment. Other reasons maybe are caused by inefficient management of franchisor including inactive marketing strategy and inconsistent terms on franchise agreements. Franchise branding should be consistent in all geographic locations to promote growth and to be recognized by customers.

3. Be interested with franchise that has active franchisor. Avoid any franchise having previous market problem specially with it's product and currently it is being improved. The interest of the market is usually swayed from existing brand to another good brand based on negative experience. The certainty of future return on investment is low. Introduction of franchisor of its franchise in new territories are good indicators of future success in your franchise investment. Other growth indicators that you should identify: acquisition of related and support businesses, partnership with leading franchise holding companies overseas, etc.

4. Check the franchise terms specially on uniform training upon start-up of business franchise operation and during years of business operation including introduction of new marketing strategy, procedures and store equipment from year to year. Identify the source of financing for any available store improvement specially on advertising strategy changing from time to time.

5. Identify the options available to franchisees on products being distributed to the stores of franchisees. There should be centralized source of products and shouldn't be requiring you to establish your own local sourcing warehouse e.g. raw materials. Calculate the time that you'll spend on local product sourcing. If there are available local suppliers related to franchisor's business, buying a franchise maybe feasible.

6. Check also the legal agreements franchisor requires from every franchisee, identify restrictions and policies that are favorable to you as a future franchisee. Check fran-

chisor's offers on responsibilities to franchisees such as long-term support and the cost of such support. Check the franchisor's experience on providing support to franchisees.

7. Compare total franchise fee with the size of business franchise and the available products to be sold or service to be provided. Prepare a comparison table, list the popular brands and their total franchise fees, calculate the difference of your target franchise compared to the franchise fees of the leading franchisors. If the difference isn't substantial, it is advisable to franchise a leading franchise brand. Establishing a new franchise brand name may take time compared to the leading franchises, franchise fee of a new brand name of franchise should offer a large discount fee compared to popular franchises.

8. Check the originality of the products of your prospective franchise if the products are patented and not common, products

could be available from different wholesalers and the concept of your prospective franchise is a form of non-centralized retailing. Buy a franchise that promotes originality of its products and each product should have a separate patent.

9. Double check if your capitalization is only enough for small franchises *e.g. food carts*, make sure that you'll be interested keeping such type of franchises. It means you have to save more fund for larger investment *e.g. fast food store*.

CHAPTER 2: FRANCHISING ADVANTAGES

Starting up a new business with your own business idea may take time and the phases until profitability may take several years of branding, marketing, advertising and other introductory strategies to create a niche in a market, usually a new business ends up into closure as a result of capital shortage.

Franchising is a form of business investment that offers a quick return on investment in a short period of time. Franchisor assures the franchisee of a certain return provided the franchisee should pay the required franchise fees. The operation system is already established and operating effectively compared to your business idea to be put up, operation procedures should be tested on efficiency and effectiveness. In franchising, only your operating company to operate the franchise should be put up. If you want to own a franchise without involving a partner or incorporating a company, a sole proprietorship company is what you need to register in your territory. Every franchise provides manual of operation including uniform procedures of producing certain products or services to maintain the quality of franchise. In your other business, you have to think to find ways of improving the performance of your business, in franchising, franchisor provides assistance on improving operation of your franchised business.

Another advantage of franchising a brand is that you can expect big sales during the pre-operating phase of your franchise compared to a newly opened business idea. It may take time to make your marketing and advertising strategies will bring in customers.

Franchisor provides regular updates to its franchisees, operation department meets regularly with franchisees to discuss marketing strategies and important improvements that franchisees should implement uniformly.

Profitable franchises are usually providing public disclosures about their financial status including the annual sales, management conditions, growth in the number of franchisees. Visit websites of popular franchises to have understanding about franchises terms, specially the budget on initial franchise fees and percentage of periodic royalty.

If your investment fund isn't sufficient to buy the franchise you desire, open a business that you like if your fund is really too far away from the ideal investment fund for franchising. Franchisors usually start from business ideas prior to branching out and eventually franchising their brands. That's why customers usually think that every store of a franchise is a branch of a large company. Franchising is the fastest way to multiply stores and to occupy territories around the world with the help of the franchisees, the buyers of franchisor's franchise. With franchising popular brands can be brought around the world and customers don't have to travel overseas just to have a bite of a stick of french fries.

Franchisor should have at least several branches prior to opening the business for franchise and the business operation should have a complete documentation of operation and should be improved within the existing branches before inviting buyers of franchise. Manual of operation should also document administrative aspect to promote uniformity in managing a franchise business. Check the website of your prospective franchisor and review the organization, operation and the terms of franchise being offered.

Popular brands aren't just franchising to anybody around the world, they also review the prospective buyers and predict the business growth of their brands. Each of the franchisors with international brands expects that more units of franchise can be purchased and stores can be opened in a specific country of a prospective franchisee. Holding more stores under franchise of a franchisor is the best expectation every franchisor dreams to have in a specific territory.

As a franchisee you should conduct review of a prospective franchise, make sure that it is a popular brand, available anywhere in your country. If it is a popular brand with numerous branches and stores under franchise in other country, find the possible reason why the brand isn't franchising in your locality, determine if you should put up a company to enter into having agreement with the prospective franchisor, identify the roles you should play, maybe a holder of several franchised stores of such franchisor. Find a way to become an operator of franchisor's branches and being a franchisee of various franchised stores at the same time in your region.

Being a franchisee you should show concern on your franchise to be considered in the renewal of your contract with the franchisor. Show responsibility in the management of your franchise, maintain the franchise's value based on its operation manual that every franchisee should use on operating and managing the business under franchise.

As a franchisee under contract with the franchisor, you are required to pay the franchising fees and periodic royalty based on the terms of agreement with regular visit or review from the operation department of the franchisor. It's a small percentage of royalty share from your annual sales or income while you're enjoying the benefits of marketability of franchisor's brand.

As a franchisor, franchising is the fastest way to bring your brand around the world without so much of capitalization, royalty income and other franchising fees can be invested in establishing branches in your desired locations. The best actions to do as a franchisor, you should develop your first few branches, improve the operation system, improve your management and ensure every aspect of your business complete and ready for franchising. Ensure also that your business visions include going globally aside from fulfilling your basic mission of doing the main purpose of your business.

Franchising brings the fastest way of world development, franchises occupy the business places without so much of thinking from the franchisees as they see every business place is occupied of the same competing brands under franchise. Franchising creates massive development around the world, usually the fast food chains as examples, investors are no longer thinking about feasibility of business, franchises are considered investment opportunities to hold with.

Popular franchises with wide market coverage usually possess trademarks that are patented and unique individually and well protected of every intellectual property agency where the franchisors' main offices are located.

If you're a new franchisee, be hesitant on giving a chance to a franchisor that hasn't established branches, there must be examples of growth prior to franchising, branching is almost similar to franchising, evaluate every branch if the business fits for franchise.

A good franchisor should provide study of a prospective location wherever every franchisee is located, if the place of franchise is rejected, the franchisor can provide suggestion of a new place where the franchise can be marketable. Another good thing about franchising is that, construction of a franchised store can be started anytime and can be finished within the agreed period, business can start immediately and completely as if a new branch is opened in a new location by franchisor. Marketing updates are provided by franchisor's team that should be uniformly implemented by franchisees. Marketing strategies of leading franchises can change quickly compared to other brands, new products can be introduced to franchisees periodically.

CHAPTER 3: TIPS ON SELECTING THE BEST FRANCHISES

Franchising is a ready business opportunity not requiring years of business experience and expertise. Everything will be prepared by franchisor including the training of sales team and managers. Operation of business is based on a well-documented manual, marketing and advertising activities are being performed by franchisor, operation team of franchisor provides non-stop support on operation and management matters, sales and banking systems that are based on the latest technology uniformly used by franchisor's branches and franchisees, inventory management system, etc.

Prepare your investment fund for franchisor's review, leading brands are reviewing prospective franchisee if you can pay immediately the franchise fees and reviewing at the same time conflict of interest of existing franchises you are holding. It is advisable not to buy more than one franchises from the same type of franchise (e.g. fast food chains). The best advice is to hold several franchised stores from one leading brand only to avoid conflict of interest from competing franchisors.

If your business is to be involved in manufacturing and distribution of a product licensed by a foreign trademark owner (e.g. coffee brand, soft drinks), this form of franchising is commonly known as licensing, the trademark owner is only concerned with the quality of its product under licensed. The licensee should pay the trademark owner the required fee prior to production of product under licensed. Licensor or trademark owner ensures that product quality is maintained and the royalty share from periodic sales is paid to the owner of trademark. The licensee is responsible for the operation and management of business. Licensee has the option to engage a contractor to do the manufacturing, the owner of trademark ensures that the standard of quality is maintained. The licensee has a freedom to do the appropriate marketing strategy similar or maybe different from the strategy of the owner of trademark.

Franchisees are completely dependent on the operation and management of franchisors. Procedures and strategies are checked regularly by franchisor if they are based on the uniform manual of operation and management. Freedom on operation specially on marketing strategy should not vary from what is suggested by franchisor. Franchisees are also required to submit reports to franchisor's operation team depending on the requirements of operation.

Tips on Buying a Franchise

1. Determine the main purpose of business, know its vision and mission.

2. Determine what problems or business issues the franchise is experiencing and what'll be the impact on future operation.

3. Know the business experience that you need to have prior to buying a franchise or the franchisor can provide everything including the operation and management support to franchisees.

4. Know the geographic locations of franchised stores and the potential for global expansion.

5. Know the financial status of franchisor's results of operations, positive sales and surpluses on accumulated income should encourage you to invest on franchise.

6. Determine requirements prior to accepting you as a franchisee such as establishment of an operating company to operate the franchise.

7. Know the market status of the prospective franchisor, the leading competitors, popular locations of model franchised stores and the extent of support to franchisees.

8. Determine the types of training being provided by franchisor's team and if managerial training is included.

9. Determine the inventory management, calculate difficulties of shipment and the policy on costing of products.

10. Know the recommended business places of your prospective franchisor/franchiser and the places considered to be not viable.

11. Determine the business organization of the franchisor/franchiser, corporation is most desirable to make the business more capable of expansion.

12. Evaluate your personal finance, determine the total franchise cost as your initial outlay to buy the franchise, determine also the total operating cost not included in the cost of franchise.

13. Determine if bank financing is reasonable to enlarge your franchising budget.

14. Study the prospective market place of your franchise, determine if there's an existing market based on the existence of competitors in the market place.

15. Compare the market prices of your products to existing competitors, determine if your brand is marketable regardless of prices of your products based on popularity of franchise.

16. Determine if competitors number is growing and the possibility that your franchise will experience slower demand year by year.

17. Observe other franchised brands in the

area, know the popularity of franchisees and the possible reasons of non-operation.

18. Determine the profitability of franchising during post-pandemic period (e.g. after Corona Virus period) in your target market place.

19. Know the history of any prospective franchise including its rank year by year, the leading franchise is the most profitable to buy.

20. Determine the satisfactory services and supports the franchisor/franchiser provides to every franchisee.

21. Know the satisfactory operation and management systems that attract any prospective franchisee (e.g. inventory system, sales and banking).

22. Determine the satisfactory assistance franchisor provides to franchisee such as site reservation or leasehold assistance.

23. Know the expenditures of franchisor on advertising and marketing, evaluate

popularity of any prospective franchise.

24. Read success stories of franchisees, determine if you'll become successful if you invest in the same franchise.

25. Visit franchised stores and note changing promotions and advertising, decide if the franchisor is doing its best to keep the attention of customers.

26. Note if your franchised store will be a direct competitor to a neighboring the same franchised store, determine the demand of market for the same brand in the same location.

27. Determine if the prospective franchisor/franchiser is a member of recognized international organization(s).

Making Final Decision to Franchise a Brand

After knowing the franchise it is time to

make decision of buying the franchise. Decision to buy means to accept the terms of franchise. Buying a franchise from a franchisor is a long-term investment decision, make sure that you're willing to comply with all the requirements and implement all the changes the franchisor wants the franchisees to do from time to time. View your every prospective franchise as a branch of a franchisor that you should manage based on a set of standards or manual of operation and management that should be complied uniformly. Decide on the nature of business, if you love the products of such franchise most likely you'll enjoy the business and you'll have strong interest of managing the business. Success of every business depends on you and can't be delegated to your manager. The value of time in business can be doubled by its owner but any manager can't be required to devote so much of personal time to achieve business success. Decide if you have sufficient time to manage any prospective franchise however you are motivated by the nature of business. If you're holding more businesses and franchises, you really need a manager to occupy your managing interest on each franchise.

Buying a franchise available worldwide is the best decision you can do, there's a certainty that your investment will have return in few years period compared to your business idea. Conduct research about franchises you're interested to know, compare the brands and decide on what franchise is the most popular and available internationally with thousands of branches and franchised stores. Check your personal finance if the initial franchise fee is within your budget and other expenditures after starting-up can be met. If your investment fund isn't sufficient to buy a franchise from the first five leading franchises, settle on other franchises that are also available internationally. Determine growth in number of stores yearly, select franchise that has more growing franchisees every year.

CHAPTER 4: THE COST OF FRANCHISE AND PERSONAL FINANCE

After making final decision to franchise a brand it's time to consider and review the cost of franchise and the source of your money to finance the franchising. The most desirable source of financing a franchise decision is your investment fund. Bank financing can be considered to increase your fund or as an additional source financial inflow in the future. The best decision to franchise should be when your investment fund is doubled in size compared to the total cost of buying a franchise. Franchising is a form of investment during the fair days that you should consider and to maintain a peace of mind instead of having a bank loan to pay resulting from your investment decision, it should be your personal finance coming from your investment fund. If your fund is doubled, there's still sufficient fund to be used in operating the franchised business.

To maintain the good feeling of investing into a profitable investment, personal finance should have sufficient balance of fund to meet the future expenditures of your franchise. The worry of return on investment can be reduced by efficient management or storekeeping, maintaining the value of assets, preventing rapid depreciation and wastage. An operator of franchises should think that investment money fund is only converted into assets and the net value of assets can be sold ten times its net value. If the franchises that you hold are brands belonging to the leading brands depending on what categories of business they belong, surely there's a return on investment in few years period.

There are costs to consider in buying a franchise: *Initial Franchise Fee, Store Construction and leasehold Costs, Cost of Initial Inventory, Cost of Training, Business Budget and other initial business costs.*

Initial Franchise Fee

Franchisor is selling its brand that will immediately benefit the franchisee and because of that reason initial franchise fee is paid at a price higher than expected by franchisee. The brand being franchised is already established and other franchisees are already profiting from the existing business of franchisor, the same reason why it is being offered to future franchisees at a high price. Initial franchisee fee not including other fees, would mean the licensing fee to use the brand of franchisor.

Store Construction and leasehold Costs

Finding a suitable location may take time plus the time to take in constructing the franchised store. This cost is added to the initial franchise fee, inclusive of store equipment and other assets. Leasehold can be a separate cost unless you own the place where the franchised store will be located.

Cost of Initial Inventory

It is usually included in the franchise fee the cost of initial inventory to be available after the store construction is accomplished. The initial balance of inventory should be reflected in the inventory management system of the franchised store.

Cost of Training

The franchise fee also includes cost of training, during the start-up period of your franchise, training is being conducted by franchisor's operation team based on the uniform manual of franchisor's operation. This training is being conducted for free in the future to meet the needs of franchisee's for operational training.

Business Budget and other initial business costs

That's why it is advisable to buy a franchise when your investment fund is twice the size of the total initial franchise fee to meet the future business budget such as budget of operation and management. There are other expenditures to pay that are considered to be fixed costs: electricity, water, etc., these expenditures aren't included in the total initial franchise fee.

Personal Finance

It is advisable that upon buying a franchise you should use your investment fund compared to borrowing it from a lending company. Franchise is a form of investment that can provide you a fast return on your investment. Park your money in this type of investment and make sure that you maintain its value and it must generate profit to make the value of your net assets doubled.

An established franchise can give assurance that your money investment can be returned to your fund in a short period of time. Then after your fund is ready to buy another the same franchise from the same franchisor, it's then the right time to open a new franchised store with the same brand.

Buying a franchise is a personal decision involving your investment fund, invest your money in a franchise that you like to have. Buy a franchise that you believe can give you an immediate return on investment. The best advice is to buy the most popular brand of franchise with worldwide franchises if your investment fund is sufficient and with balance for future business expenditures.

Popular or leading brands of franchises are those brands that have proven market success, with operation and management systems that are considered to be leading in the industry of franchising. Leading franchises have operation manuals that are being implemented uniformly by franchisees. Popular franchises have worldwide popularity and almost everyone in the world knows about the brand. Marketing is no longer your responsibility, the interest of customers may sway from one leading brand to another depending on the marketing strategies of your franchisor. The franchisor's operation team is responsible for the brand's popularity and market patronage.

Although there's a regular franchise fee to be paid to the franchisor, there's an assurance that sales of your franchised store can absorb the franchise fee after netting the operation and management periodic expenditures.

CONCLUSION

Thank you for the time you've spent on reading this ebook titled "BUSINESS START-UP: FRANCHISING". I hope you've gained wisdom from reading this ebook.

In addition to a regular franchise fee being paid to franchisor, there's a situation that the franchisee is contributing to a group advertising expenditures depending on the advertising strategies being employed by your franchisor. On the other hand, franchisor can fix competitions between franchisees in a specific territory, a franchisee can be given an exclusive right to operate a franchise in a specific location separated and distant from other franchisees.

Make sure that you will read carefully every detail and the terms of franchising contract. Make clarification if you're in doubt about the terms of franchise agreement that you're signing. Get the help of a law firm to ensure that the agreement of franchise is mutually beneficial both to franchisee and franchisor. Get a contract for every franchise that you are buying from the same franchisor.

There's a situation that a franchisee is granted the authority to become a master franchisee in a specific country, where such authority is granted the right to establish branches or to sell franchise on behalf of the franchisor.

Franchisor protects itself from direct competition of its franchisees by preventing you as a franchisee of establishing the same type of business with intention to franchise the same and to make yourself a franchisor of the same type of business.

There's a clause in a franchise agreement stating the percentage of royalty payable to franchisor, this royalty is also known as commission or share of your franchisor from your periodic sales, net profit or net income.

If you are a franchisee and having a unique business or your own started-up business idea, you have the option to franchise your own brand after considering conflict of interest with your franchised brands. Franchising is the fastest way of going global with the help of your future franchisees. Building your net worth and capitalizing based on your surplus income will take time. Save years of waiting by franchising your brand. Building an empire of brand around the world will need large amount of investment fund and leveraging with bank loans. Franchising is the only way of building an empire of brand attracting talented and well-funded investors or business people around the world. Using the talents and capital of others will make you a successful future franchisor.

ABOUT THE AUTHOR

Dell Navarro

Previously a Business and Management Consultant of his own registered Consulting Company for years. A registered Accountant. Stockholder of various Corporations. Copyrighted author of business books.

BOOKS BY THIS AUTHOR

Business Start-Up: Managing The Business

Business Start-Up: The Sales

Business Start-Up: The Plan Of Business

Business Start-Up: The Online Marketing

Business Start-Up: Branding

www.ingramcontent.com/pod-product-compliance
Lightning Source LLC
Chambersburg PA
CBHW070858220526
45466CB00005B/2033